Jobs If You Like...

Music

Charlotte Guillain

www.raintreepublishers.co.uk
Visit our website to find out more information about Raintree books.

To order:
☎ Phone 0845 6044371
▤ Fax +44 (0) 1865 312263
▣ Email myorders@raintreepublishers.co.uk

Customers from outside the UK please telephone +44 1865 312262

Raintree is an imprint of Capstone Global Library Limited, a company incorporated in England and Wales having its registered office at 7 Pilgrim Street, London, EC4V 6LB – Registered company number: 6695582

Edited by Rebecca Rissman, Daniel Nunn, and Adrian Vigliano
Designed by Steve Mead
Picture research by Mica Brancic
Originated by Capstone Global Library
Printed and bound in China by South China Printing Company

ISBN 978 1 406 24069 6 (hardback)
16 15 14 13 12
10 9 8 7 6 5 4 3 2 1

British Library Cataloguing in Publication Data
Guillain, Charlotte.
Jobs for kids who like music.
780.2'3-dc22
A full catalogue record for this book is available from the British Library.

Acknowledgements
We would like to thank the following for permission to reproduce photographs: [select]

Cover photograph of [select] reproduced with permission of [select].

We would like to thank [name of organization or individual] for [pronoun] invaluable help in the preparation of this book.

Every effort has been made to contact copyright holders of material reproduced in this book. Any omissions will be rectified in subsequent printings if notice is given to the publisher.

Contents

Some words are shown in bold, **like this**. You can find out what they mean by looking in the glossary.

Why does music matter?

Do you play a musical instrument or enjoy singing? Or maybe you just love listening to music? Music is all around us every day on the radio, on the television, and on the Internet.

Music is an important part of many people's lives.

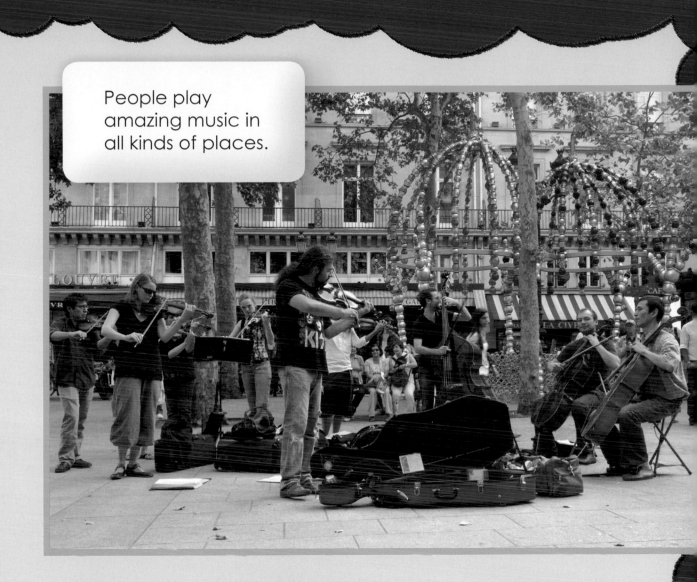

People play amazing music in all kinds of places.

We listen to music to relax, to dance, and to make us happy! It's fun to play and sing with other people and **entertain** an audience. There are many different jobs that involve music in all sorts of ways. Read on to find out more!

Be a music therapist

Does music sometimes change the way you feel? If you were a music **therapist**, you would use music to help people to feel better. You might cheer people up by helping them to play instruments or sing together.

Many music therapists work with disabled children.

Music therapists can use music to make people happier.

Music therapists need to know how to play musical instruments very well. They also need to be good at talking and listening to people. They enjoy helping people to have fun making music.

Be a sound engineer

If you like working with gadgets and **equipment** then maybe you could be a sound **engineer**. Sound engineers work in a **recording studio**, using equipment to record music and other sounds for radio, film, television, and websites.

Sound engineers learn to use lots of special equipment.

Sounds engineers need to know about different types of music. They need to be able to hear very well and have a good sense of **rhythm**. They work with different people all the time.

Sound engineers help musicians to make the best sound as they play.

Be a composer

If you like making up your own music and songs then you could be a **composer**. Composers can write music for orchestras or rock bands. Some composers write music for advertisements or computer games.

Many composers include lots of different instruments in their music.

Composers are usually very good musicians and enjoy playing music. Sometimes they use computers to help them write new music. It can take a long time to write a new piece of music.

Composers experiment with different sounds as they write new music.

Be a musical agent

If you were a musical agent, you would listen to lots of singers and musicians. You might find them on the Internet. You would find the best **performers** and help them to get work. You might help someone to become a star!

All sorts of musicians work with musical agents.

Singers and musicians need agents to help them make the right choices.

Musical agents need to be able to spot the best performers. They help their **clients** by organizing their work. They help singers and musicians decide where to work and what songs to perform.

Be a professional musician

If you are very good at playing an instrument or singing then maybe you could be a professional musician. You might play in live concerts with an orchestra. You could make recordings for people to listen to on the radio or television, or to download.

Only the best musicians can play in a professional orchestra.

Professional musicians spend a lot of time learning and practising new pieces of music. They need to take good care of their instrument or voice. They work in new places and with different people all the time.

Many professional musicians work in theatre.

Be a performing artist

If you were a performing artist, you would work hard recording and performing songs. You might write your own songs or play songs your manager chooses. Often bands and singers are only popular for a short time.

Some performing artists get to make music for huge crowds of people!

Session musicians enjoy working with many different people.

Session musicians play with different bands when they need extra musicians. They can work with lots of great bands and singers. They are usually very talented musicians who can play many musical styles.

Be a DJ

If you were a DJ, you might play music and talk on the radio. Other DJs play music for people to dance to in clubs. You would need to know a lot about music and choose the best songs for the people listening.

Radio DJs work in a studio with lots of special equipment.

DJs need to know how to use lots of different **equipment**. Sometimes they make their own sounds and add effects to the music. They need to have plenty of energy and a good sense of **timing**.

DJ is short for disc jockey.

Be a promotions manager

Are you good at talking to people? Maybe you could be a promotions manager. It would be your job to tell people about a band or orchestra's music and concerts. You would talk to **journalists** about the musicians.

Promotions managers make sure everyone knows about a new song or concert.

It's important for bands to be on television to tell people what they are doing.

Promotions managers sometimes work for a record company. They might arrange **photo shoots** for a singer or band. They try to get their musicians on the television or in the newspapers.

The backstage crew

If you like travelling and listening to live music, then you could be part of a band's backstage crew. You would help to set up concerts and other events. You might set up musical instruments or organize the sound or lighting **equipment** for a concert.

The backstage crew who set up the stage are called "roadies".

The backstage crew have to pack the equipment away carefully after a show. It is hard work, with lots of late nights and travelling. But they see lots of bands playing live!

The backstage crew make sure everything is working properly during a show.

e a music producer

If you were a music producer, your job would be to arrange the recording of a band's songs. You might help a new band record a demo so they can sell a song to a record company.

Music producers talk to a band about how to make their music sound better.

Music producers often choose the sound **engineers** and studio for a recording. They might suggest changes to the music or **lyrics** of a song. They help choose which songs to include on a band's new album.

Music producers help a band make the finished songs that we hear.

Choosing the right job for you

When you decide what you want to do when you grow up, don't just think about school subjects. Think about what you enjoy doing. If you don't want to work late at night then you wouldn't like being backstage crew!

If you are very good at playing music or singing then you might be able to perform. It isn't easy and very few people do this for a living. But there are many other interesting musical jobs and there should be something to suit everyone.

Five things you couldn't do without music

- Dance
- Go to concerts
- Enjoy exciting films
- Learn to play an instrument
- Sing

Music job chart

If you want to find out more about any of the jobs in this book, start here:

	Backstage crew	Composer	DJ	Music producer	
You need to:	Be strong and hardworking	Have lots of ideas for new music	Know a lot about music and bands	Be good at explaining your ideas	
Best thing about it:	Listening to great live music!	Hearing people play your music!	People dancing to your music!	Seeing your recording top the charts!	

	Music therapist	Popular musician	Professional musician	Promotions manager	Sound engineer	Musical agent
	Be able to play several instruments	Be very determined	Be very good at playing an instrument or singing	Be good at talking to people	Be able to hear different sounds	Go to lots of concerts and listen to lots of bands
	Making people happy!	Having a number one song!	Hearing the audience clap!	Seeing your band on television!	Making a song sound fantastic!	Finding a new star!

Glossary

client person who pays another person to work for them

composer person who writes new pieces of music

engineer person who uses science and maths to make tools, buildings, and machines

entertain show an audience something interesting

equipment something made to be used in a special way

journalist person whose job is to collect news and information and share it with people on television, radio, and in newspapers

lyrics words to a song

performer person who sings, dances, or acts for an audience

photo shoot session where a photographer takes lots of photos of people

recording studio special place where music is recorded

rhythm regular sound pattern

session musician musician who sings or plays instruments with bands for recordings or performances

therapist person who is trained to help people using special treatment

timing knowing when to do something

Find out more

Blast

www.bbc.co.uk/blast/music_audio/
Visit this website to find out more about jobs
in music.

Virtual Orchestra

ngfl.northumberland.gov.uk/music/orchestra/
default.htm
You can find out more about the instruments in an
orchestra on this website.

BBC Music

www.bbc.co.uk/music/introducing/advice/
On this website you can get more advice about a
job in music.

Index